BASEBALL LEGENDS

Hank Aaron
Grover Cleveland Alexander
Ernie Banks
Albert Belle
Johnny Bench
Yogi Berra
Barry Bonds
Roy Campanella
Roberto Clemente
Ty Cobb
Dizzy Dean
Joe DiMaggio
Bob Feller
Jimmie Foxx
Lou Gehrig
Bob Gibson
Ken Griffey, Jr.
Rogers Hornsby
Walter Johnson
Sandy Koufax
Greg Maddux
Mickey Mantle
Christy Mathewson
Willie Mays
Stan Musial
Satchel Paige
Mike Piazza
Cal Ripken, Jr.
Brooks Robinson
Frank Robinson
Jackie Robinson
Babe Ruth
Tom Seaver
Duke Snider
Warren Spahn
Willie Stargell
Frank Thomas
Honus Wagner
Ted Williams
Carl Yastrzemski
Cy Young

CHELSEA HOUSE PUBLISHERS

CAL
RIPKEN, JR.

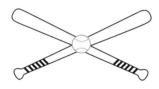

Jim Campbell, 1937 -

Introduction by
Jim Murray

Senior Consultant
Earl Weaver

CHELSEA HOUSE PUBLISHERS
Philadelphia

Cover photo credit: AP/Wide World Photo

Produced by Choptank Syndicate, Inc.

Editor and Picture Researcher: Norman L. Macht
Production Coordinator and Editorial Assistant: Mary E. Hull
Designer: Lisa Hochstein
Cover Designer: Alison Burnside

1 3 5 7 9 8 6 4 2

Library of Congress Cataloging-in-Publication Data

Campbell, Jim, 1937-
        Cal Ripkin, Jr. / Jim Campbell.
                p.   cm. — (Baseball legends)
        Includes bibliographical references (p.) and index.
        Summary: A biography of the Baltimore Orioles' shortstop
who earned the nickname "Iron Man" in 1995 when he broke Lou
Gehrig's record for most consecutive games played.
        ISBN 0-7910-4380-0
        1. Ripkin, Cal, 1960- —Juvenile literature. 2. Baseball
players—United States—Biography—Juvenile literature.
3. Baltimore Orioles (Baseball team)—Juvenile literature.
[1. Ripkin, Cal, 1960- . 2. Baseball players.] I. Title.
II. Series.
GV865.R47C46 1997
796.357'092—dc21
        [B]   97-610
                                                                 CIP
                                                                 AC

CONTENTS

WHAT MAKES A STAR

Jim Murray

No one has ever been able to explain to me the mysterious alchemy that makes one man a .350 hitter and another player, more or less identical in physical makeup, hard put to hit .200. You look at an Al Kaline, who played with the Detroit Tigers from 1953 to 1974. He was pale, stringy, almost poetic-looking. He always seemed to be struggling against a bad case of mononucleosis. But with a bat in his hands, he was King Kong. During his career, he hit 399 home runs, rapped out 3,007 hits, and compiled a .297 batting average.

Form isn't the reason. The first time anybody saw Roberto Clemente step into the batter's box for the Pittsburgh Pirates, the best guess was that Clemente would be back in Double A ball in a week. He had one foot in the bucket and held his bat at an awkward angle—he looked as though he couldn't hit an outside pitch. A lot of other ballplayers may have had a better-looking stance. Yet they never led the National League in hitting in four different years, the way Clemente did.

Not every ballplayer is born with the ability to hit a curveball. Nor is exceptional hand-eye coordination the key to heavy hitting. Big league locker rooms are filled with players who have all the attributes, save one: discipline. Every baseball man can tell you a story about a pitcher who throws a ball faster than anyone has ever seen but who has no control on or *off* the field.

The Hall of Fame is full of people who transformed themselves into great ballplayers by working at the sport, by studying the game, and making sacrifices. They're overachievers—and winners. If you want to find them, just watch the World Series. Or simply read about New York Yankee great Lou Gehrig; Ted Williams, "the Splendid Splinter" of the Boston Red Sox; or the Dodgers' strikeout king Sandy Koufax.

A pitcher *should* be able to win a lot of ballgames with a 98-miles-per-hour fastball. But what about the pitcher who wins 20 games a year with a fastball so slow that you can catch it with your teeth? Bob Feller of the Cleveland Indians got into the Hall of Fame with a blazing fastball that glowed in the dark. National League star Grover Cleveland Alexander got there with a pitch that took considerably longer to reach the plate; but when it did arrive, the pitch was exactly where Alexander wanted it to be—and the last place the batter expected it to be.

There are probably more players with exceptional ability who didn't make it to the major leagues than there are who did. A number of great hitters, bored with fielding practice, had to be dropped from their team because their home-run production didn't make up for their lapses in the field. And then there are players like Brooks Robinson of the Baltimore Orioles, who made himself into a human vacuum cleaner at third base because he knew that working hard to become an expert fielder would win him a job in the big leagues.

A star is not something that flashes through the sky. That's a comet. Or a meteor. A star is something you can steer ships by. It stays in place and gives off a steady glow; it is fixed, permanent. A star works at being a star.

And that's how you tell a star in baseball. He shows up night after night and takes pride in how brightly he shines. He's Willie Mays running so hard his hat keeps falling off; Ty Cobb sliding to stretch a single into a double; Lou Gehrig, after being fooled in his first two at-bats, belting the next pitch off the light tower because he's taken the time to study the pitcher. Stars never take themselves for granted. That's why they're stars.

1

BREAKING THE UNBREAKABLE RECORD

> "Lou Gehrig is looking down and giving
> his approval."
>
> — Joe DiMaggio

They called it Streak Week, that last week in September 1995, when the attention of the baseball world turned toward Baltimore, and the spotlight shone on the Orioles' shortstop, Cal Ripken, Jr.

Ripken was about to break one of the game's "unbreakable" records: Lou Gehrig's mark of 2,130 consecutive games played. To do this, Ripken had played in every game of every season for 14 years. It was like never missing a day of school, from first grade through senior year, and then some.

Lou Gehrig had played first base for the New York Yankees in the 1920s and 1930s. Because of his outstanding durability, he became known as the Iron Horse. He seemed indestructible, until a rare disease sidelined him in 1939, and killed him two years later.

As the record drew near, Ripken, a man who literally grew up in baseball, admitted that the attention and hype was starting to get to him. "I've been very achy the last few weeks," he said. "Maybe it's nerves. It's been a difficult time. It's been tough to sleep. Usually I sleep like a rock. But there's a

Cal Ripken, Jr. circles the field at Baltimore's Camden Yards as 46,272 onlookers and millions of baseball fans around the world cheer his record-breaking 2,131st consecutive game played on September 6, 1995. Ripken's feat high-lighted a season marred by the lingering effects of the 1994-1995 players' strike.

switch in my body that won't turn off. I toss and turn. It's been exhausting."

The Orioles' season had been disappointing. They were unlikely to earn even a wild card spot in the playoffs. But on September 5, the night Ripken would tie the record, bats exploded. Four home runs in the second inning gave the Orioles a 7–0 lead over the California Angels at Camden Yards. When the game became official after the top of the fifth inning, the Orioles came off the field as the huge numbers displayed on a nearby warehouse changed to 2–1–3–0, indicating that Ripken had tied Gehrig's record. The fans rose and began a five-minute ovation. Several times Ripken came out of the dugout, joined by his teammates, to acknowledge the cheers. The opposing Angels also paid tribute to the man everybody in baseball respected and admired; they lined up outside their dugout and applauded. When Ripken then went up to the plate and ripped a home run, the noise and celebration began all over again.

During postgame ceremonies on the field, Ripken received many gifts from sports stars and other celebrities. At a press conference attended by hundreds from the media, Ripken said, "I'm not in the business of script writing, but if I were, this would be a pretty good one." As the hour grew late, Ripken, weary from the game, the hype, and the endless flood of questions, excused himself by saying, "I have to get up early in the morning. It's my daughter's first day of school tomorrow and I want to take her."

The only numbers on anyone's mind as September 6 dawned were 2,131, the record by which Ripken would become the new yardstick for measuring the iron men of the future. There was much anticipation before the game, but nobody was more anxious to get things started than Ripken himself. "I'm looking forward to it," he said, "and I'm looking forward to the end of it, too. To be honest, the last few days have been an eternity. Every time you look at the clock, it seems to move more slowly. It's time to celebrate it and enjoy it. But I hope [the hype] doesn't linger on."

Despite the presence of many celebrities, Ripken chose two very important people in his life to throw out the ceremonial first pitch—his children, Rachel, 6, and Ryan, 2. Then, in the fourth inning, Ripken electrified the happy crowd by hitting a home run to give the Orioles a 3–1 lead.

What happened next probably has never occurred on a baseball field, and may never

Lou Gehrig (left) and Babe Ruth formed the heart of the Yankees' "Murderers Row" of the 1920s and 1930s. Gehrig, a first baseman, did not miss a game in 14 years, despite numerous broken fingers and other injuries, until a fatal illness sidelined him in 1939. He died two years later.

Ripken bats for the last time in Game 2,131. He singled and hit one of four Orioles' home runs in their 4–2 victory. The banner on the warehouse beyond right field announces the new record, which stood at 2,316 when the 1996 season ended.

happen again. Orioles second baseman Manny Alexander squeezed his glove around Damon Easley's soft pop-up to end the Angels' fifth inning and make the game official. Ripken ran for the dugout as the numbers on the high warehouse wall changed to 2–1–3–1 and Oriole Park at Camden Yards erupted. Cheers and applause cascaded down onto the field. A few times Ripken stepped out of the dugout to wave to the appreciative fans. Then he looked up into the seats to find his parents, Cal, Sr. and Vi. His eyes met his father's; they both sensed how important they were to each other as they joyously pumped their arms in the air.

Pulling off his uniform shirt as he went, Ripken walked to the box seats where his wife, Kelly, and their children were sitting. Under the uniform, he wore a T-shirt that said, "2,130+ Hugs and Kisses for Daddy." Ripken then picked up his son and gave his daughter a kiss. He walked over to a nearby seat to shake hands with Bill Ripken, his brother and former teammate.

Ripken returned to the dugout, but the fans continued to rock the ballpark with cheers, chanting, "We want Cal, we want Cal." Again, he stepped out to wave. When he ducked back into the dugout, the roar of the crowd got even louder. Teammates Bobby Bonilla and Rafael Palmeiro each grabbed one of his arms and pushed him out of the dugout, saying, "Go out and take a lap around the field. They want you. So give 'em what they want."

Ripken began trotting around the perimeter of the playing field, stopping along the way to shake hands and high-five fans. When he reached the Orioles' bullpen, he took both of catcher Elrod Hendricks' hands and held them firmly. Hendricks had been with the Orioles for all of Ripken's streak. Then he continued around the field. When he reached the Angels' dugout, their manager, Marcel Lachemann, offered a con- gratulatory hug, as did coach Rod Carew and former Oriole Rene Gonzales. Ripken's parents sat and took it all in through misty eyes.

It took 22 minutes for the celebration to die down and the game to continue. The Orioles won, 4–2, and then the special postgame ceremony started. Outfielder Brady Anderson presented Ripken with a gift from his teammates. Joe DiMaggio, who had played for the Yankees with Lou Gehrig, spoke, assuring Ripken that even the greatest records were made to be broken, and that "Lou Gehrig is looking down and giving his approval."

Ripken spoke last. He acknowledged fans everywhere, then named "the four most important people in my life": his mother and father and wife, and Eddie Murray, a veteran player who had been Ripken's mentor when he first came up to the major leagues.

Ripken concluded, "I know that if Lou Gehrig is looking down tonight, he isn't concerned about someone playing one more consecutive game than he did. Instead, he is viewing tonight as just another example of what is good and right about the great American game.

"Whether your name is Gehrig or Ripken, DiMaggio or Robinson, or that of some young star

Ripken received his biggest—and most tearful—hug of the night from clubhouse assistant Butch Burnett, who was often the butt of Ripken's pranks and impromptu wrestling matches. Ripken is as admired and liked by other players as by Baltimore fans.

who picks up a bat and puts on a glove, you are challenged by this game to do your very best day in and day out. And that's all I ever tried to do."

The press conference and interviews went on until two a.m. When it was all over, Bryan Johnson, a fan who had caught Ripken's home run ball, presented the memento to the new iron man. "It should be Cal's," he said. An appreciative Ripken signed one of his bats for Johnson with the inscription, "Now we both have something to share the memory."

2

BORN TO PLAY BALL

"If somebody beat me, it used to make me so mad."

— Cal Ripken, Jr.

Calvin Edwin Ripken, Jr. was born into a baseball family on August 24, 1960 in Havre de Grace, Maryland. His father, Cal Senior, and Uncle Bill were minor league players. His mother, Violet, had been a softball star in high school.

Cal's father was not there to greet his first-born son. He was a catcher for the Baltimore Orioles' farm team in Fox Cities, Wisconsin at the time. But his manager, Earl Weaver, who would later manage young Cal at Baltimore, gave Senior time off to see Vi, their year-old daughter, Ellen, and his new son.

Minor league ballplayers live nomadic lives. Every spring they leave home to go to spring training, then report to a different city or town for the baseball season. The newlywed Vi had stayed home and worked in Aberdeen, Maryland during her husband's rookie season in 1957. They could not afford to be together on his $150 a month salary. But after that Vi and the children went everywhere that Senior went.

When he was in the sixth grade, Cal, Jr. wrote, ". . . before I was a year old, we journeyed to Daytona Beach, Florida; Thomasville, Georgia;

Cal Ripken's first boyhood idol was Baltimore's legendary third baseman Brooks Robinson. A Hall of Famer on and off the field, Robinson was known as the human vacuum cleaner, winning 16 Gold Gloves in his 23 seasons. He holds almost every career fielding record for third basemen.

17

Little Rock, Arkansas; Leesburg, Florida; and Rochester, New York."

A shoulder injury ended Senior's playing days and he became a manager in the Orioles' organization. By the time he could walk, young Cal knew the sounds and smells and sights of the tiny dugouts and clubhouses and grandstands of dusty minor league ballparks. As soon as his hands were big enough to hold a ball and glove, he was seldom without them.

The young Baltimore farmhands his father managed, including future stars like Jim Palmer and Mark Belanger, soon got used to seeing the toddler on the field, asking questions and pestering them to roll the ball to him.

By 1965 there were four Ripken children. Vi Ripken drove Ellen, Cal, Fred and newborn Billy 3,000 miles across the country to Kennewick, Washington, where their father was managing the team. Cal later recalled, "We'd pass the time singing or playing word games. If we needed to stretch, sometimes we'd find a ball field and take family batting practice." They got as far as Lubbock, Texas by Easter Sunday. Ellen and Cal fretted that the Easter bunny would not know how to find them at their motel, but they awoke to discover that they had not been overlooked. On the way home after the season, the family visited Yellowstone National Park, the Badlands of North Dakota, and Mt. Rushmore.

Most of the minor league players on Senior's teams were too young to have families, so the Ripkens made few friends with other kids on their travels. This brought them closer together, but it also made them fierce competitors in the games they played. Whatever they played, Cal had to be the best. "If somebody beat me," he later recalled, "it used to make me so mad. The whole house heard about it."

They were all good athletes; Cal and Billy made it to the big leagues, Fred was just as good but never pursued it, and Ellen became an outstanding softball third baseman who could "really rifle that seed," as her father described her throwing ability.

Cal Senior was an excellent teacher, and young Cal asked a lot of questions. At the games, while other kids were running around or playing in the dirt, Cal studied the action intently, watching how the players did things at bat and in the field. Afterward he would ask his father to explain the strategies of the game.

Wherever he managed, Senior put on clinics for young players in the area, showing them how things were done at the professional level. Cal was usually on hand, absorbing everything. Years later, when he was a minor leaguer himself, Cal would pull off some "inside baseball" trick. When his dad asked where he learned it, Cal said, "From you, at one of your clinics somewhere."

Spending his summers in minor league towns, Cal seldom saw a big league game. The young players on his father's teams became his heroes. "I never thought much about the big leagues," he said. "You know how most kids pick their heroes, play in the back yard and pretend to be some famous big league player? Well, for me it was different."

Cal dreamed about being a ballplayer, but not about being a big leaguer. Just being a professional like the boys who played for his father would be enough. One afternoon when he was 12, an incident almost ended all his dreams. Senior was managing in Asheville, North

Ripken's father, Cal, Sr., was a minor league player and manager during Junior's youth. Later he coached and managed the Orioles. An excellent teacher, he developed many of the Orioles' stars during his 35 years in the organization.

Carolina. Junior was on the field practicing with third baseman Doug DeCinces and some other players. Suddenly the sound of rifle shots cracked the air. Bullets whizzed by the players, kicking up dirt near their feet. The quick-thinking DeCinces grabbed Cal and threw him into the dugout. Nobody was hurt, but DeCinces said, "I'll never forget it. That's how close it was." They never found the person who fired at them.

Cal played on his first Little League team that year in Asheville. He started out as a catcher like his dad, but soon switched to pitching and playing the outfield. The next year his team won the state championship and advanced to the Southeast Regional tournament. Although they did not advance any farther, it was a positive experience for Cal and his teammates. "That was the biggest thrill of my life," he wrote in an eighth grade essay.

Eventually Cal did pick a big league hero. It was the same one millions of other youngsters chose—Brooks Robinson, the Orioles' All-Star and future Hall of Fame third baseman. Cal had seen enough of him to appreciate his greatness.

Robinson had also seen enough of Cal to appreciate his potential. Said the man they called Mr. Oriole, "He was always around the ballpark. He lived and died baseball. I know guys are supposed to like baseball, but some are special. It's almost a sin if they don't play. The thought of not playing every inning of every game never crosses their minds. That's the way the game was meant to be played. That was young Cal."

A GOOD FOUNDATION

"Don't take me out. Please."
— Cal Ripken, Jr.

In many ways, Cal Ripken, Jr. was not like most youngsters growing up. Because of his dad's job, he often found himself in minor league ballparks with his father. The professional players were his friends and teachers. But in some ways he was like the average American boy. After he played Little League, he advanced to Babe Ruth League and Mickey Mantle League. He did all this while moving from place to place as his father's career dictated.

Cal recalled his dad was rarely able to see him play. "Baseball took my dad away from me. He left at one o'clock every day on days the team was at home, and he was gone completely half the time when the team was on the road. If I wanted to see my dad I learned that I'd have to go to the ball-park with him. We'd watch from the stands. I'd sing along with the fans at the start of the game and during the seventh inning stretch. On special days we'd go on the field for a picture."

As Cal got older, he would go early with his father to the ballpark, where his father would give him a uniform and send him to the outfield, warning him, "Don't come into the infield. It's too

Junior gets an approving look from his mother, Vi, after signing a four-year contract with the Orioles in 1984. With his father away every summer, Vi was his biggest rooter throughout his Little League and high school careers.

dangerous. Shag flies, and always keep your eyes open."

But when Cal was playing, his mother was always there for him in his father's absence. She took him to practices and games, and sat in a lawn chair behind the backstop. Often she had a Thermos bottle of Kool-Aid, and always she had words of encouragement.

The competitive toughness that made Cal such a durable and reliable player showed early in his life, but he could also be funny sometimes without meaning to be. Once he was pitching and having trouble with his control. He hit three or four batters in a row. The coach called time out and went out to the mound to try to settle him down, but quickly returned to the bench, laughing. He explained to Vi Ripken, "When I got out there, your son looked at me and said, 'They don't get out of the way very fast, do they.'"

While baseball separated father and son, soccer brought them together. When baseball season was over, Senior served as Junior's coach in an Aberdeen soccer league. Cal enjoyed the time with his dad. "He'd tell me baseball stories from his playing days and about the toughness of his old baseball teammates. Being together, though, is what counted."

In ninth grade, Cal tried out for the high school varsity baseball team. The coach, Don Morrison, asked the prospective players to run a mile in less than six and a half minutes. Part of the group could not make it and dropped out. Others ran so slowly they had no hope of finishing under 6:30.

As Morrison recalled, "One little kid [Cal was 5-foot-7 and weighed 128 pounds] came up to me. He was red in the face and panting hard.

He said, 'Coach Morrison, I just can't do it today. May I come back tomorrow and try again?' That was the first time I saw Cal Ripken, Jr."

Graduation losses from the previous season gave Cal an opening and he made the team as a second baseman. Morrison remembered him as being special. "His presence on the field was exceptional and he had gifted hands when it came to fielding ground balls."

At bat Cal struggled in his first year. He grew about three inches and gained 20 pounds between seasons. However, that was not big enough when he collided with Steve Slagle, a player for Elkton High who was 6-foot-5 and weighed 270. Cal was covering second base one day when Slagle, the Elkton Express, roared into second. Taking the full force of the burly baserunner in his rib cage, Cal went airborne for a few seconds. He landed and was gasping for breath when Morrison reached him. Showing his coach the spirit he would later show the world, Cal pleaded, "Don't take me out. Please."

By the time Cal reached the 11th grade, his father was a coach with the Orioles in Baltimore. Young Cal was now a rangy six-footer and he was pitching when he was not playing shortstop. Thanks to his contacts with major league pitchers, he had developed a variety of pitches to go with an 86-mile-an-hour fastball. Most scouts and bird dogs (part-time scouts) who saw him rated him as a pitcher. But one Orioles scout, Dick Bowie, saw something more in Cal. The other scouts would be standing around waiting for Cal to come in and pitch, but Bowie was more interested in Cal as an infielder.

In the summer of 1977, Cal's Mickey Mantle League team reached the World Series in

Sherman, Texas, but they came up short of the championship.

In school, Cal was a serious student. He always gave his best effort in class and graduated with a 3.5 average, including a difficult course in calculus.

In his senior year, Cal had grown to 6-foot-2 and weighed 185 pounds. He won 7 and lost 2 as a pitcher, striking out 100 batters in 60 innings. One major league scouting report said, "Built like and has Jim Palmer-like actions." Palmer, an Orioles pitcher at the time, became a Hall of Famer. Despite Cal's batting .492 that year, no other scouts shared Dick Bowie's opinion of him. When Cal threw a two-hitter and struck out 17 for Aberdeen High to win the state Class A championship, they were even more convinced that pitching was Cal's future. They also felt the Orioles had the inside track on signing him because of his father's connection with the team.

Doug DeCinces rescued 11-year-old Cal from a sniper's bullets during practice one day at Asheville, North Carolina, where Cal, Sr. was the manager. DeCinces took over third base for the Orioles when Brooks Robinson retired; in 1982 Ripken replaced DeCinces.

On June 6, 1978 the Orioles selected Cal in the second round of the annual amateur draft. He was the 44th player taken. The Orioles were in California when Senior heard the news. He called his wife and said, "We had a son drafted today." Vi Ripken, who had seen more of her son's career, replied, "Oh, I've known it would happen for months."

A week later, Cal signed for a $20,000 bonus and $500 a month. His dad drove him to Baltimore, where he met another new rookie, Tim Norris. The young, aspiring major leaguers departed for Bluefield, West Virginia and the Orioles' rookie farm team in the Appalachian League.

4

THE CLIMB TO
THE MAJORS

"Believe in your talents and listen to
  your heart."

— Cal Ripken, Jr.

When Cal Ripken, Jr. arrived in Bluefield on June 15, 1978 he and other young rookies quickly realized they were not the big guns anymore. They were just ballplayers. And nearly everyone on the team was as good as the next guy, or at least had as much potential.

Ralph Rowe, the Bluefield batting coach, knew how they felt. "For the first time they felt pressure," he said. "They were always the best on their team. But now they were playing for money and everyone here was as good as the next."

Even though Orioles favorites like Don Baylor, Boog Powell, Bobby Grich, Mark Belanger, Doug DeCinces and Eddie Murray had begun their careers in Bluefield, the young players faced long odds. Only about one in 10 would advance to the major leagues.

Still, Cal stood out. He had been around ballplayers for so long, he had gained a maturity on the field that the others lacked. John Shelby, a Bluefield teammate, and Cal hit it off. They became friends, and Shelby quickly pegged Cal.

Cal Ripken's professional baseball career began in 1978 in this ballpark in Bluefield, West Virginia in the Appalachian Rookie League. Ripken spent four years in the minor leagues, with stops at every level, before reaching the majors.

"He was a young kid, very skinny, but very talented. He never wanted to come out of a game. He came to play, and that meant it all."

Cal got off to a rough start, but then began hitting the rookie league pitching. He played in 63 of the 70 games and batted .264, but he did not hit a single home run. It was the only year in his long career that he failed to hit one over the fence. In the field he made a discouraging number of errors, but the advice of his father rang in his ears: "Always remember that no matter what happens on the field, you deserve to be there. Always believe that you belong."

Years later, Cal looked back on his rookie year fondly. "It was the most fun I had in baseball, because we were all the same. As you go up and up, it gets to be more of a job."

In 1979 Cal climbed another rung of the ladder, to Miami in the Class A Florida State League, where he had a good year. His fielding at third base and shortstop improved and he batted a solid .305 with a league-leading 28 doubles. In August he was called up to Charlotte, North Carolina in the Class AA Southern League. He hit the ball well in batting practice and decided he would be a home run hitter. He hit three in 17 games, but had only eight other hits and batted .180. That taught him a valuable lesson: concentrate on meeting the ball and the home runs will take care of themselves.

Cal returned to Charlotte for the 1980 season. At 6-foot-4 and weighing 200 pounds, he was considered too big for a shortstop. The position was usually played by a smaller man. In fact, when he reached the major leagues, he became the tallest man ever to play the position for a lengthy career. Later, he had some advice

for young players who may not fit the exact mold
that scouts or coaches were looking for. "Don't
let what others say keep you from reaching your
potential. Believe in your talents and listen to
your heart."

Cal worked long hours on his fielding, taking
hundreds of ground balls and working on turning the double play. He practiced baserunning
and getting a jump on the pitcher to steal a base.
His time of 4.2 seconds from home to first base
was good for a player of his size.

At Charlotte he developed into a power hitter,
blasting 25 home runs and 28 doubles while
batting .276. When the season ended, he played
winter ball at Caguas in Puerto Rico. The next
spring he went to his first big league training
camp, in Miami. Writers covering the Orioles
considered him a good prospect to open the
season as the Baltimore third baseman and
maybe even capture Rookie of the Year honors.
But the Orioles did not like to rush players; they
preferred to develop them slowly and thoroughly.
So they assigned Cal to Rochester in the AAA
International League, where his father had played
and managed. Before he left, Orioles manager
Earl Weaver told him, "See you soon."

Early in the season Ripken looked like one
of the great sluggers of all time. In one April game
he hit three home runs. In May he blasted two
3-run shots. But the one game Cal remembered
most began on Saturday, April 18 in Pawtucket,
Rhode Island. After 9 innings the game was tied,
1–1. After 22 innings, it was tied, 2–2. By that
time it was well past midnight and Easter Sunday had nearly dawned. At 4:07, with the score
still at 2–2 after 32 innings, the game was
suspended. When the game was resumed in

June, Pawtucket scored in the 33rd inning to win the longest game in history.

Better pitching at the AAA level, just below the majors, actually made Ripken a better hitter. He applied all the knowledge he had gained during the summers with his father in the lower minor leagues to figure out pitchers' patterns instead of just guessing what was coming. He hit .288 with 23 home runs and 31 doubles, and won the Rookie of the Year award. When he got the news, he said, "Wow, that's great. It makes it worth all the hard work you put in."

A players' strike interrupted the 1981 major league season. Few games were played in June and July. When there was talk of minor leaguers being called up to replace the striking players, Ripken said he would not cross the picket line and play. The strike ended on August 8 and Ripken was called up by the Orioles. Being in the big leagues meant that he could once again ride with his father, an Orioles coach, from their home in Aberdeen to Memorial Stadium.

Cal made his major league debut on August 10 as a pinch runner for Ken Singleton, who had doubled. When John Lowenstein singled, Cal dashed home with his first big league run. On August 16 Cal started at shortstop and got his first major league hit, a single off Chicago pitcher Dennis Lamp. He got into a few more games as a pinch hitter and runner. Cal then packed his bags and headed back to Caguas for another season of winter ball.

No matter where he was playing, Cal never wanted to come out of a game. One hot day in Puerto Rico the temperature soared over 100 degrees. The manager, Ray Miller, called for Ripken to sit down, but Cal refused.

Meanwhile, back in Baltimore the Orioles made some moves that paved the way for Ripken to take his place in Memorial Stadium. They traded their third baseman, Doug DeCinces, and shortstop Mark Belanger left to sign with the Los Angeles Dodgers. Cal Ripken was penciled in as their future third baseman.

Mark Belanger, shown here turning a double play, played catch with the 4-year-old Cal when Belanger was the last regular Orioles' shortstop before Ripken moved into the position midway in the 1982 season.

5

BIG LEAGUE ROOKIE

"Just go out there and do what you can,"
— Reggie Jackson

When Cal Ripken, Jr. signed his first major league contract in February 1982, he mentioned two goals he had set for himself: "The first is to get to the big leagues, and the second is to stay there and do well. I've achieved one part, and I'm not going to stop now."

He opened the season as the Orioles' third baseman on April 5 against Kansas City. On his first trip to the plate, with Ken Singleton on base, he faced right-hander Dennis Leonard and launched a drive over the fence for a two-run homer. Later he said, "I could hardly believe it, and I didn't go into my home run trot. I almost jumped into the air and then really flew around the bases. Singleton was just jogging in front of me and when he got to home plate, I was right on his heels." He added two more hits in the Orioles' 13–5 win.

Many years later, Cal said, "If I had to pick out the most exciting day of my career, it would be that opening day in my rookie year. There were 50,000 people in the stands, and my family was there, with my father coaching third base."

But things did not go as smoothly as that first game in the weeks that followed. Ripken fell into a slump that got deeper and deeper. The worse it

Ripken's consecutive game streak is all the more amazing because he played the most demanding infield position. Here he leaps to avoid the spikes of the sliding Darryl Sconiers while making the throw to first for the double play. He missed only 164 innings in 14 years.

got, the more he pressed. The more he pressed, the lower his batting average sank. Then one day words of encouragement came from an unexpected source. They were playing the California Angels, and action stopped while Orioles manager Earl Weaver argued with an umpire about a close call. The Angels' star slugger, Reggie Jackson, was on third base. During the time out, he turned to Ripken and said, "Hey, I want to talk to you. I know you can play. Just go out there and do what you can. Do what got you to the big leagues, and everything else will take care of itself."

Another who helped was the Orioles first baseman, Eddie Murray, who batted fourth behind Ripken in the lineup. "When I was slumping," Cal recalled, "Eddie helped me. When he had come up to the majors and didn't know any players, he had felt out of place, so he knew what I was going through." Murray and Ripken became very close friends.

In early May Ripken was batting just .117. On May 2 he was batting against Mike Moore of Seattle. Moore threw a fastball that came right at Ripken's head. Too late to duck out of the way, he turned his head and the ball banged off his helmet. Down he went. Weaver and Cal Senior rushed to him. They saw a hole in his helmet as big as the ball. Junior was not badly hurt and asked to stay in the game. However, Weaver thought it best to take him out. His teammates joked to the struggling rookie that "at least that was a way to get on base."

Beanings can have long-range effects on some hitters, causing them to become gun-shy at the plate, but the experience had the opposite effect on Ripken. He broke out of his slump and by season's end was batting .264. He led all rookies with 23 home runs and 93 runs scored and easily won Rookie of the Year honors.

On May 29 Ripken played third base in the first game of a doubleheader. In the second game, Weaver replaced him with Floyd Rayford. That was the last game Ripken would fail to start until Lou Gehrig's consecutive game record was passed.

The Orioles tried several shortstops that year but none satisfied Weaver. He decided to move Ripken to short until the Orioles could find someone better for the position, allowing Ripken to return to third base. The switch from third to short came as a surprise to Ripken. Weaver had not said anything to him about it; he just wrote Ripken's name on the lineup card at shortstop and put it up on the clubhouse wall. When Junior saw it, he went to his father, who told him, "Don't worry. Just catch the ball and throw it to first."

The Orioles toured Japan for a 14-game exhibition series in 1984. Here Ripken (right) and pitcher Mike Boddicker pose with three young Japanese fans. Baseball is as popular in Japan as in the United States.

Weaver then told him, "I just want you to catch the ball, take your time, and make a good throw to first. If he's out, he's out. If he's safe, he's only on first base."

Fourteen years later the Orioles were still looking for a shortstop good enough to move Ripken back to third base.

With four games to play the Orioles were three games behind the first place Milwaukee Brewers. They took both ends of a Friday doubleheader and won again on Saturday, but the Brewers won the pennant with a victory on the last day. Earl Weaver retired when the season ended and Joe Altobelli took his place in 1983.

Confident that he could improve on his first year, Ripken got off to such a good start in 1983 he was selected to the American League All-Star team. It was an awesome experience for the young Oriole. "I felt good enough to be there," he said, "but I was looking around the locker room at guys I used to root for as a kid. You say, 'Oh, God, how do I belong in this group?' and then you say,' I'm here, aren't I? I must belong.'" The Americans won for the first time in 12 years.

Ripken and the Orioles got hot in September and pulled away from the East Division. The clincher came in Milwaukee, and Cal Senior, who for 27 years had never allowed himself to celebrate a victory, poured a can of beer over Junior's head. "I guess the father in me finally came out," he said.

After dropping the first game in the ALCS to the Chicago White Sox, the Birds took the next three, led by Ripken's .400 batting. In the World Series they quickly dispatched the Philadelphia Phillies in five games. Eddie Murray's two home runs paced the Orioles to a 5–0 win in the finale.

The last out was made on a line drive right to Cal Ripken who snared it and broke into a big grin.

Ripken had batted .318 with 27 home runs for the world champions, which earned him the league's Most Valuable Player award.

In accepting the trophy, he said, "Most valuable player isn't something you aim for. By the same token, though, you want people to know about you. I'd like to be someone the kids would like to grow up to be like, to emulate in the backyard games. You have to be careful to be really good in their eyes. They model themselves after you."

Joe Altobelli said, "I've seen a lot of players over the years who reminded me of other players, but I've never seen one like Cal."

To Ripken, this was the way baseball was supposed to be. He looked forward to winning many more world championships, and to playing every inning, every game, every day for 20 years.

6

DAY IN, DAY OUT—
YEAR IN, YEAR OUT

"If the good Lord wants Cal to have a day off, He'll let it rain."

— Johnny Oates

Onetime Yankees manager Casey Stengel once said, "I don't like them fellas who drive in two runs and let in three."

The Orioles had always stressed defense and Ripken made that his priority for 1984. He had made 25 errors the year before and felt that was too many. He succeeded beyond his own hopes, setting a record with 583 assists. His hitting did not suffer; he batted .304 with 27 home runs, but the Orioles failed to make the playoffs.

In May 1985 Ripken set a team record, held by his boyhood idol, Brooks Robinson, by playing in his 464th consecutive game. It was a record he almost missed. On the second day of the season, he tried a pick-off play and his spikes caught on the bag. He heard a pop and felt a sharp pain in his left ankle. The trainer, Richie Bancells, taped it tightly, but the next day the ankle looked like a soccer ball. The Orioles had a day off, and played an exhibition game at the Naval Academy. The next day the swelling had gone down and Ripken played.

The 1991 All-Star Game was the Cal Ripken Show. He won the home run hitting contest on July 8, and hit a game-winning three-run homer in the third inning the next night, which earned him the All-Star MVP trophy.

He was still years away from Lou Gehrig's record, but people connected with the team began to speculate about it. Marty Conway, then a vice president of marketing for the Orioles, recalled, "That was the first time anyone spoke of the streak as one that could approach Gehrig's, but most of the talk was confined to the team. Not much was said publicly or in the media. Then Rick Vaughn, the public relations director, began to include it in the media notes he handed out to writers and broadcasters."

By the end of the year the streak was at 603 games, but Ripken was more concerned over the Orioles' failure to make postseason play again. Having won the World Series in his second year, he had assumed that he would see action in many more postseason series. But it was not turning out that way.

In 1986 the Orioles finished seventh; their record was under .500 for the first time in 19 seasons. Ripken continued to perform consistently at bat and in the field, batting his usual .282 and hitting 25 home runs. That year he met Kelly Geer and they began dating. On New Year's Eve the young couple went out on the balcony of Ripken's home. Kelly saw Christmas lights in the yard that spelled out, "Will you marry me?" They were married in November 1987.

Shortly after the 1986 season, Cal Senior was named the Orioles manager. He was only the third man ever to manage a team that his son played for. During spring training, writers asked him what it would be like to manage his son. In his no-nonsense way, Senior said, "Our association on the field has always been professional. He knows my job and I know his."

On July 11, Bill Ripken was called up by the Orioles to play second base, and Senior now had the distinction of managing two sons on the same big league team. By late August Ripken's streak had reached 883, but he was in a slump. He and his father came in for heavy criticism. Some experts thought Junior was hurting the team by playing every day and not hitting. They blamed Senior for hurting the team by not giving his son a rest. Frank Robinson, a coach who had been a Hall of Fame player, defended the Ripkens. "There's no blueprint to get out of a slump," he

In 1987 Cal, Sr. became the first to manage two sons on a major league team. Cal's younger brother, Bill, at left, played second base. Senior was fired after the Orioles lost the first six games of the 1988 season; the Orioles went on to lose a record 21 before posting a win.

said. "Some guys rest, some forget batting practice. Others do like Rip, and they play their way out of it."

Ripken continued to start every game, but his father surprised everyone on September 14 when he took Junior out of a game, ending his streak of consecutive innings at 8,243. "It was a surprise to be taken out," Ripken said, "but I didn't feel I was owed an explanation. The manager's job is to make moves. It just happens, in this case, the manager is my father."

Ripken's hitting slipped to .252, although he continued to maintain a 25-plus home run production, rapping out 27.

By now Ripken was an established star with a high salary, which he shared with community projects like the Baltimore School for Performing Arts and adult literacy programs. He was also aware of his consecutive games streak and eager to keep it going, not so much to strive for the record as to demonstrate his ardent conviction to do his job every day, no matter how he felt. He knew that he would have to take special pains to stay in top condition 12 months a year. He talked with Nolan Ryan, who pitched until he was 46, and Carlton Fisk, who had caught more games than any other catcher at that time. They told him of the importance of off-season conditioning. Ripken listened and devised a workout routine that suited his needs. He built a home that included a gym with a regulation size basketball court, a weight room and batting cage.

When the Orioles lost their first six games in 1988, Cal Senior was fired as manager. Frank Robinson replaced him, but the Orioles' record sank to 0–21. They went on to lose 107 games and finish seventh. Ripken hit more than 20 home runs for the seventh year in a row.

The streak continued to add up in 1989, passing Steve Garvey's third-longest run of 1,208 games. But it was another disappointing year for Ripken. He batted just, .257 although the Orioles climbed to second place.

The Orioles had another long, disappointing season in 1990. On June 22, Ripken played in his 1,300th game, breaking the mark of Everett Scott. Now only Gehrig's 2,130 stood between him and the record. But because the Orioles were playing so poorly, when Orioles' public

Despite the stress of dealing with the intense media pressure as the streak neared the record in 1995, Ripken never stopped signing autographs before and after the games, often staying to pose and visit and sign for fans hours after the other players had gone home.

address announcer Rex Barney announced the record to the crowd at Memorial Stadium, the fans booed. Ripken finished the year with his lowest batting average so far—.250.

Ripken's managers always defended his playing every day, even when he was not hitting, because of his fielding. They insisted that his glove alone made him an All-Star. Ripken had made only eight errors in 1989. Through July of 1990, he set records for shortstops by handling 431 chances in 95 games without an error. In 1990 he made only three errors, for a record fielding average of .996. He was determined not to be one of those "fellas" Casey Stengel had talked about, who let in three runs for every two they drove in.

Ripken silenced all his critics in 1991, batting .322, knocking out 34 home runs and driving in 114 runs. His honors that year included Player of the Year, the All-Star Game MVP, his first Gold Glove at shortstop, and his second American League Most Valuable Player.

His ninth consecutive All-Star Game provided one of the few highlights of the otherwise losing season for the Orioles. Invited to participate in the pregame Home Run Derby, Ripken thought he did not belong on the field with sluggers like Cecil Fielder. He wound up winning the contest with 12 smashes into the seats; his last was a drive that landed in the fifth deck of Toronto's SkyDome. In the game the next day, he hit another rocket into the seats to give the AL a 3–1 lead in the game they won, 4–2. He gave the van he won as the All-Star MVP to a Baltimore reading program.

The Orioles opened the 1992 season in their new ballpark, Oriole Park at Camden Yards, and climbed to a third place finish. As Ripken's hitting slumped to .251 and his home run total fell below 20 for the first time, the cry went up again to give him a day off. But manager Johnny Oates refused, saying, "If the good Lord wants Cal to have a day off, He'll let it rain." In August Ripken signed a five-year contract with the Orioles for more than $30 million.

The three Ripken Orioles were torn apart in 1993. Cal Senior was released as a coach and Bill was given his release as a player. Bill signed with Texas and rejoined the Orioles in 1995, but Senior retired from the game. Ripken was hurt by the departure of his father and brother, but he was determined not to let it affect his performance on the field, and to rebound from his disappointing year. He was now in the superstar class, but remained a low-key star.

"He doesn't do it with a lot of flash," said Johnny Oates. "He doesn't run around high-fiving everybody...he just plays the game. He is a superstar who wants to be treated as the ordinary person that he is."

On June 6, 1993 Ripken's streak survived another scare. In a game against Seattle at Camden Yards, some inside pitches sparked a fight between the teams. As Ripken charged in to help break it up, his spikes caught in the grass and he twisted his right knee. It swelled up so much overnight he doubted that he could play the next day. The trainer worked on it all that day and just before the game Ripken tested it gingerly in the clubhouse. When he found he could put his weight down on it, he played that night.

As the streak lengthened, Ripken did not change the way he played the game. He went at it with the same intensity, never shying away from a situation that might result in an injury. He knew that if he did things halfway he was more likely to end up getting hurt.

On July 26 his second child, Ryan, was born. Ripken did not have to miss a game to be present at the birth; the Orioles happened to have an off day that day.

Rumors of a possible players' strike grew stronger as the season went into August. The Players Association and the club owners were unable to agree on a new contract governing the

Two-year-old Ryan Ripken practices swinging from the left side as his dad and sister, Rachel, look on. On the morning of the record-breaking game on September 6, Ripken was up early to take Rachel to her first day of school.

game. The players set a deadline of August 12, and when no agreement was reached, everything stopped. Even then, nobody expected the interruption to last more than a few weeks, but August limped into September with no settlement in sight. Then it became too late to resume a pennant race with any meaning. The owners cancelled the rest of the season and the playoffs, and for the first time in 90 years there was no World Series.

Ripken had bounced back to hit .315 and keep the Orioles in the pennant race; they finished second to the Yankees. The streak stood at 2,009 games when baseball closed its doors early. It was now 10 years since Ripken had played in a World Series, something he thought would happen many times during his career.

7

THE STREAK
GOES ON

"I just love to play baseball."
— Cal Ripken, Jr.

Baseball's club owners and striking players had not reached an agreement when the 1995 season was set to open. Teams planned to use replacement players, minor leaguers and amateurs who had come to training camps hoping for a chance to play. Cal Ripken would have been forced to cross the picket line and play, something he said he would not do, or see his streak stopped. Games played with replacement players would count as official games.

But the owner of the Orioles, Peter Angelos, refused to hire any replacement players. He said the Orioles would not take the field for any games without Ripken and the regular players, even if it meant that they would forfeit every game of the season.

Fortunately for Ripken and all of baseball, the owners abandoned the idea of using replacement players at the last minute. The season opener was delayed until April 26, but the regular players were back on the field.

Players and fans consulted calendars and schedules to figure out when the record-breaking game would occur. Provided there were no rainouts,

Veteran first baseman Eddie Murray became Ripken's friend and mentor when Cal broke in with the Orioles in 1982. Murray left the team in 1989, but he returned in 1996 in time for Cal to congratulate him when Murray hit his 500th home run on September 6, 1996. Murray's 500 home runs and 3,000 hits is equaled only by Willie Mays and Hank Aaron.

Like Cal Ripken, Jr., Lou Gehrig was a quiet hero, admired by all for his character and dedication. Twice an American League Most Valuable Player, Gehrig had a career batting average of .340 and hit 493 home runs before his career abruptly ended at the age of 37.

the big series would take place at Camden Yards against the California Angels September 4, 5 and 6.

To help celebrate the event, huge banners were hung on the Baltimore & Ohio Railroad warehouse that loomed just outside the ballpark behind the right field bleachers. They first went up on August 29 with the numbers 2–1–2–2. At the middle or the end of the fifth inning of each game, a new number was unfurled, the fans would cheer Ripken, and he would tip his cap to them. For the first seven games of Streak Week, the Orioles were behind in the score when the games became official, and Ripken was on the field when the numbers changed. The monstrous scoreboard screen would show a closeup of him, repeatedly saying "Thank you" to a crowd that could not hear because of its own cheering. Ripken tried not to smile; it was not his style. He also tried not to cry as the ovation thundered around him.

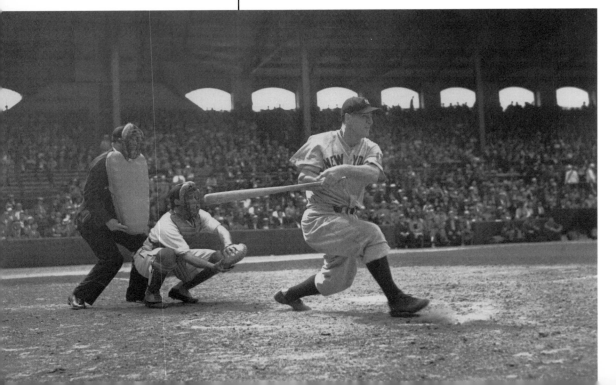

Even opposing teams saluted the iron man shortstop. When game 2,128 became official, the Seattle Mariners stood on their dugout steps and applauded Ripken along with the rest of the sell-out crowd. When the Angels came to town they did the same. One of the Angels was Rex Hudler, who had once played second base alongside Ripken for the Orioles. "Every one of the Angels wanted to run over and give Cal a high five," he said, "but we had to remember the integrity of the game."

Realizing how special the streak was for the fans as well as Ripken, the Orioles made special preparations for game 2,131. Usually, ushers tear tickets in half when fans present them at the turnstile. On September 6, with a sense of history, the ticket takers carefully stamped the tickets, leaving the fans with a whole ticket as a souvenir of the historic event.

With Ripken's approval, 260 special on-field seats were set up for the record-breaking game. Each seat cost $5,000, raising more than $1 million for Johns Hopkins Hospital's research toward finding a cure for the disease that had killed Lou Gehrig.

Ripken had been uncomfortable with all the attention he had drawn wherever the team played all season. He looked forward to things returning to normal. He may have recalled the note his wife, Kelly, had left for him at the start of the season: "Enjoy the year. Let everyone tell you how great you are." He had heard it enough to last a lifetime. While he enjoyed the festivities, he was relieved when game 2,132, then 2,133 and so on came along.

The 1996 season opened as usual with number 8—Cal Ripken, Jr.—at shortstop. After a slow start under new manager Davey Johnson, the team dueled with the Yankees for the East Division lead. Gradually, the Yankees pulled away, and it looked as if the Orioles might not even qualify for the wild card spot in the playoffs. Through it all Ripken was hitting well. His fielding was as good as the league's top shortstops. At midseason, he was again chosen to play in the All-Star Game.

What pitchers, hitters, baserunners, Father Time and Mother Nature could not do to Ripken, a fellow American League All-Star—pitcher Roberto Hernandez—almost did. While lining up for the All-Star team photo, Hernandez slipped. He threw out his arms to keep his balance. His flying elbow caught Ripken on the nose and broke it. Ripken had it treated and did not even miss the All-Star Game.

By late August, the Birds were in the thick of the fight for the wild card spot, battling the Mariners and White Sox. Ripken powered his 21st home run of the year and had three more hits to lead the Orioles to a key 10–5 win over the Mariners and move within a half game of the White Sox.

Late in the season the Orioles made a trade that brought Eddie Murray back to Baltimore. Ripken was pleased with the move, calling Murray "the biggest influence in my career." When Murray rejoined his old team he was close to a milestone of his own—500 home runs. He reached that goal exactly one year to the day after Ripken had broken Gehrig's record, September 6, 1996. Ripken was as happy for his old friend as he had been for his own achievement.

Although the Orioles cut down the Yankees' 12-game lead to 2 games, they could not catch New York. But with Ripken, Murray and others hitting well, and some fine pitching, they did claim the wild card place and returned to post-season play for the first time since 1983.

The Orioles faced the Cleveland Indians in the division series. The Indians, who had lost the 1995 World Series to the Atlanta Braves, were heavy favorites. But the Orioles outplayed them and ended the best-of-five series in four games. Ripken batted .444 in the series, and made many superlative plays in the field. More than once the television announcers called for replays to illustrate the remarkable fielding ability of the 36-year-old shortstop. In one game he made a dazzling stop that he could not have reached if he had been any shorter than his 6-foot-4, as if to say "How about that" to those who had called him too big to play shortstop.

But Ripken missed a chance to play in his second World Series when the Yankees came to town and swept the Orioles out of the picture. New York then went on to defeat the Atlanta Braves for the championship.

Through the years many commentators had marveled at Cal Ripken's durability. They knew he took good care of himself. They knew about his strict off-season conditioning program. They knew he was strong and intelligent. But they wondered how he had managed to avoid any crippling injuries, playing a position that put him in the middle of more action than any other player except the catcher. Hundreds of players had spent time on the disabled list since he had reached the major leagues, yet he had not missed a game and rarely missed an inning. There was some luck involved, but there was more planning than anything else.

Rick Vaughn, former Orioles public relations director, explained, "Cal is such a student of the game, he has reduced it to a science. He has studied baseball so long and so well, he knows the risks involved in each play or situation, and he knows how to avoid placing himself in a position where he might be at risk. You seldom see him make a reckless play.

"He'll give it his all, but he's not about to needlessly put himself in harm's way. This is not to say he shies away from anything or anyone—he doesn't, but he knows exactly where to be and how to play it. He can turn a double play and never be knocked over by a take-out slide; he simply knows what to do and where to do it. That comes from instinct and practice, practice, practice. Cal has worked for everything he's got.

"I've never seen anyone close to him when it comes to studying the game that way. There's a very good reason he's played in all those games. Study and playing through pain are a strong part of his make-up."

It was almost 2:00 a.m. when Ripken and his wife, Kelly, met the media after the post-game ceremonies following Game 2,131. The next day 300,000 fans turned out for a parade honoring Ripken and the team.

Ripken and his family remained deeply committed to the community with reading and literacy their special interests. During the 1996 season attractive cards of Ripken were passed out by the thousands. The front of the card featured a color photo of him batting. The back had an important message from him: "Being able to read enhances everyone's life. Not only will it open many doors for you, but it will also broaden your horizons. It's an adventure every time you open a book."

Following the long 1996 season, Ripken went to Japan for his second visit with an All-Star team that included teammate Brady Anderson. Despite an injured right hand, Ripken played in every game of the eight-day tour. And he played as hard as he ever did in any playoff or World Series. Asked why he did so, he said, "I just love to play baseball."

CHRONOLOGY

1960   Born Calvin Edward Ripken, Jr. August 24 in Havre de Grace, Maryland

1978   Signs with Baltimore Orioles

1981   Plays in longest game in baseball history while with Rochester
       Makes major league debut August 10 as pinch runner

1982   Begins streak of consecutive games played on May 30
       Named Rookie of the Year

1983   Voted American League Most Valuable Player

1987   Marries Kelly Geer November 13

1991   Wins second Most Valuable Player Award

1995   Breaks Lou Gehrig's record on September 6 by playing in 2,131 consecutive games

1996   Starts record 13th straight All-Star Game at shortstop
       Ends season with streak at 2,316 games

MAJOR LEAGUE STATISTICS

BALTIMORE ORIOLES

YEAR	TEAM	G	AB	R	H	2B	3B	HR	RBI	BA	SB
1981	BAL	23	39	1	5	0	0	0	0	.128	0
1982		160	598	90	158	32	5	28	93	.264	3
1983		162	663	121	211	47	2	27	102	.318	0
1984		162	641	103	195	37	7	27	86	.304	2
1985		161	642	116	181	32	5	26	110	.282	2
1986		162	627	98	177	35	1	25	81	.282	4
1987		162	624	97	157	28	3	27	98	.252	3
1988		161	575	87	152	25	1	23	81	.264	2
1989		162	646	80	166	30	0	21	93	.257	3
1990		161	600	78	150	28	4	21	84	.250	3
1991		162	650	99	210	46	5	34	114	.323	6
1992		162	637	73	160	29	1	14	72	.251	4
1993		162	641	87	165	26	3	24	90	.257	1
1994		112	444	71	140	19	3	13	75	.315	1
1995		144	550	71	144	33	2	17	88	.262	0
1996		163	640	94	178	40	1	26	102	.278	1
Totals		2381	9217	1366	2549	487	43	353	1369	.276	35

WORLD SERIES

YEAR	TEAM	G	AB	R	H	2B	3B	HR	RBI	BA	SB
1983		5	18	2	3	0	0	0	1	.167	0

FURTHER READING

Thornley, Stew. *Cal Ripken, Jr.: Oriole Ironman.* Minneapolis: Lerner Publications, 1992.

Macnow, Glen. *Sports Great Cal Ripken,* Jr. Hillside, NJ: Enslow Publishers, 1993.

Nicholson, Lois. *Cal Ripken, Jr.: Quiet Hero.* Centreville, MD: Tidewater Publishers, 2nd ed., 1995.

Ripken, Cal Jr. *Count Me In.* Dallas: Taylor Publishing Co., 1995.

Ripken, Cal Jr. Ripken: *Cal on Cal.* Arlington, TX: Summit Publishing Group, 1995.

INDEX

PICTURE CREDITS
AP/Wide World Photo: pp. 8, 20, 22, 26, 34, 40, 45, 50, 58; Bluefield Orioles: p. 28; National Baseball Library and Archive, Cooperstown NY: pp. 11, 16, 37, 43, 52; Norman L. Macht: p. 56; Photo File: p. 2; Richard Lasner: p. 12; Ric Riggins: pp. 14, 48; UPI/Bettmann, p. 33

JIM CAMPBELL is a native of Pennsylvania and a graduate of Susquehanna University. Sports have been important to him for much of his life. In high school and college he participated in football, basketball, baseball, and track and field. He has been director of the Little League Baseball Museum, a game-day assistant with the Pittsburgh Steelers, historian at the Pro Football Hall of Fame, research editor with NFL Properties, and director of communication with the NFL Alumni. He is currently the Director of Athletic Development—the Bison Club—at Bucknell University in Lewisburg, Pennsylvania, and writes a weekly column for *Pro Football Weekly* and other magazine articles. His "Golden Years of Pro Football" has gone into a second printing. He is also the author of "The Importance of Joe Louis." Campbell and his wife, Brenda, live in Selinsgrove, Pennsylvania.

JIM MURRAY, veteran sports columnist of the *Los Angeles Times*, is one of America's most acclaimed writers. He has been named "America's Best Sportswriter" by the National Association of Sportscasters and Sportswriters 14 times, was awarded the Red Smith Award, and was twice winner of the National Headliner Award. In addition, he was awarded the J. G. Taylor Spink Award in 1987 for "meritorious contributions to baseball writing." With this award came his 1988 induction into the National Baseball Hall of Fame in Cooperstown, New York. In 1990, Jim Murray was awarded the Pulitzer Prize for Commentary.

EARL WEAVER is the winningest manager in the Baltimore Orioles' history by a wide margin. He compiled 1,480 victories in his 17 years at the helm. After managing eight different minor league teams, he was given the chance to lead the Orioles in 1968. Under his leadership the Orioles finished lower than second place in the American League East only four times in 17 years. One of only 12 managers in big league history to have managed in four or more World Series, Earl was named Manager of the Year in 1979. The popular Weaver had his number, 5, retired in 1982, joining Brooks Robinson, Frank Robinson, and Jim Palmer, whose numbers were retired previously. Earl Weaver continues his association with the professional baseball scene by writing, broadcasting, and coaching.